The Inside-Outside Book of LONDON

ROXIE MUNRO

UNIVERSE

Published by Universe Publishing
A Division of Rizzoli International Publications, Inc.
300 Park Avenue South
New York, NY 10010
www.rizzoliusa.com

© 2015 Roxie Munro

2015 2016 2017 2018 / 10 9 8 7 6 5 4 3 2 1

Printed in China

ISBN-13: 978-0-7893-2913-4

Library of Congress Catalog Control Number: 2014952739

To my husband, Bo

The British Museum

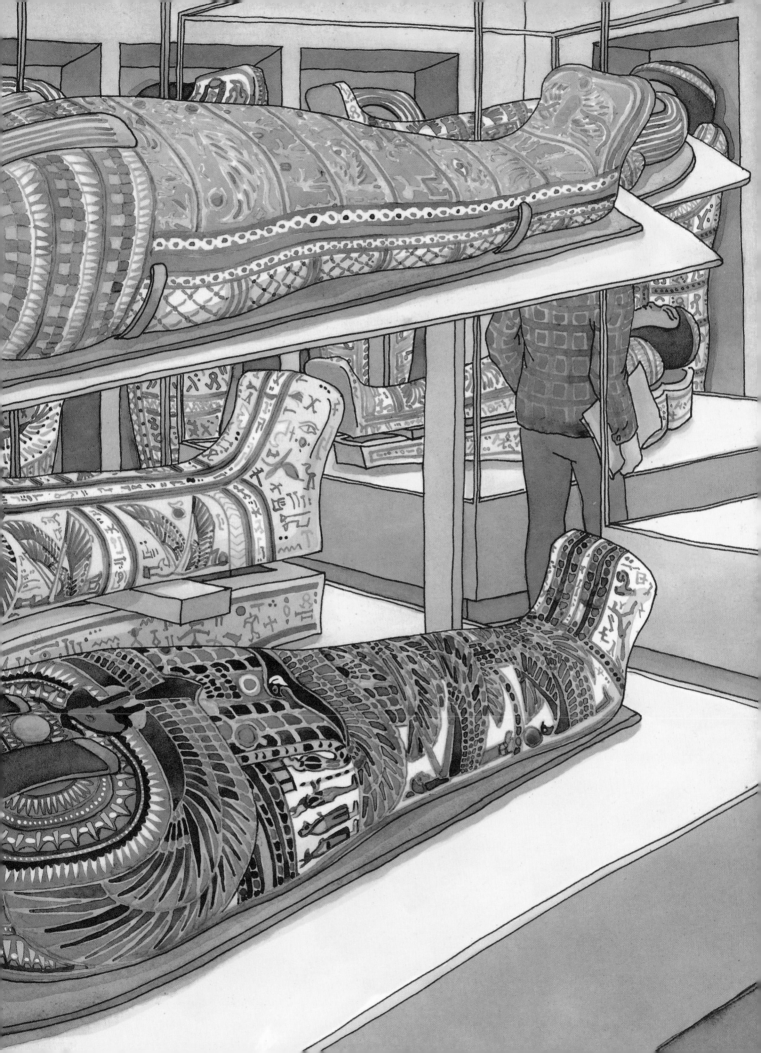

Waterloo Station

New Oxford Street

to Trafalgar Square via Regent Street

Shaftesbury Avenue

Buckingham Palace

The Houses of Parliament

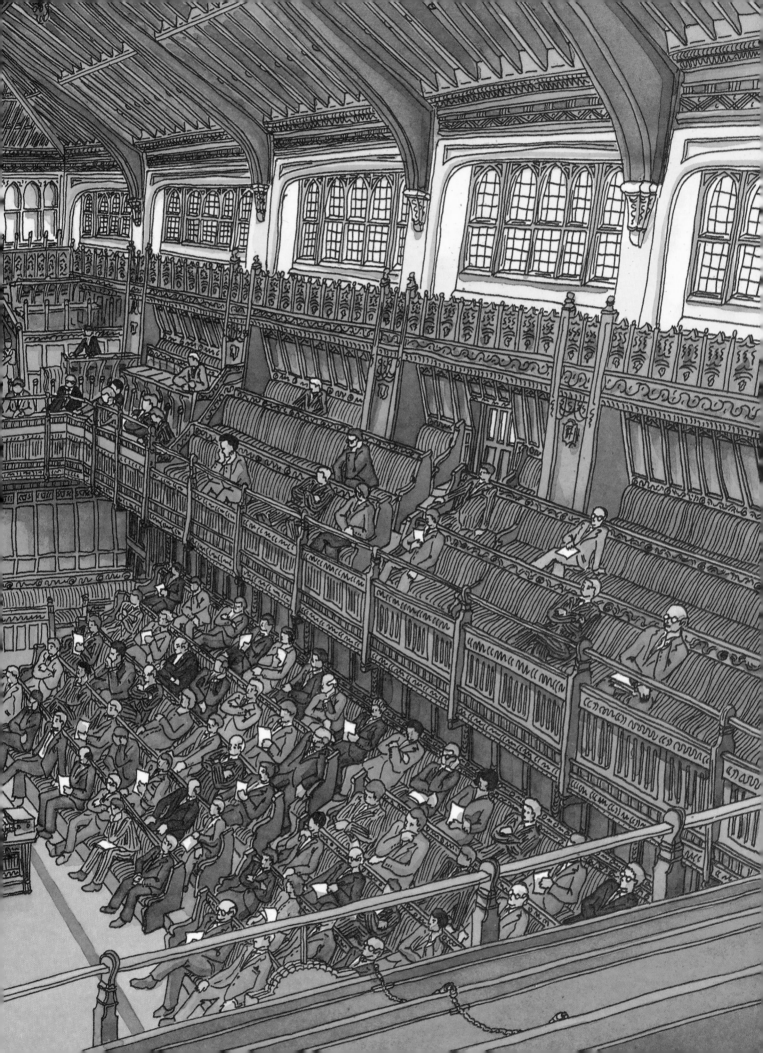

The Tower of London

St. Paul's Cathedral

Although the clock in the Elizabeth Tower of the Houses of Parliament is popularly called BIG BEN, the name actually refers to the 13½-ton bell upon which the hours are struck. The clock, still wound by hand, has four faces, each one 23 feet wide, with roman numerals two feet high and minute hands 14 feet long. This much-loved London landmark began service in 1859 and keeps nearly perfect time today; old coins are added or subtracted to the mechanism to make whatever tiny adjustments of weight are necessary.

The TOWER BRIDGE—built to harmonize with the Tower of London, which it adjoins—opened in 1894 as the only moveable bridge across the Thames River. All of the original machinery for raising and lowering the drawbridge is still in place, although the early steam engines have been replaced by electric motors. Several times a week the bridge is raised so that tall ships can pass through. The towers, 800 feet apart, are connected by a latticework pedestrian footbridge 60 feet above ground level. The view from the walkway looking west includes the Tower of London (on the right), the City (an important one-mile-square commercial area), and the South Bank (on the left).

THE BRITISH MUSEUM houses the richest and most varied collection of treasures in the world, including the Rosetta Stone (which enabled scholars to translate Egyptian hieroglyphics) and sculptures from the Greek Parthenon. The main entrance, completed in 1852, is located on Great Russell Street in Bloomsbury. The popular Egyptian mummies, many of which are between 4,000 and 5,000 years old, include human mummies of all ages as well as mummies of cats and other animals. The museum is free and open every day.

Located on the south bank of the Thames River, WATERLOO STATION opened in 1848. It serves the southern region of England and is the busiest of London's 10 mainline rail terminals, handling more than 94 million passenger entries and exits a year. It is the London terminus of the tunnel under the English Channel. As a train approaches Clapham Junction, the most active rail intersection in Great Britain, a suburban scene is visible from the window.

NEW OXFORD STREET, a continuation of Oxford Street, is a thoroughfare dense with shops. It marks the southern boundary of the area known as Bloomsbury. James Smith & Sons has been manufacturing umbrellas, walking sticks, seat sticks, sword sticks, and whips for more than 180 years. Made-to-order sticks and umbrellas are measured to the customer's height and are cut from a wide variety of woods (chestnut, ash, apple, maple, ebony, and rosewood) with unusual handles (tortoiseshell, carved wood, animal heads, and even gadgets).

London's instantly recognizable red double-decker buses are an excellent way to take in the city's sights. The route pictured goes down REGENT STREET, one of the most fashionable shopping streets in the world, then through Piccadilly Circus to TRAFALGAR SQUARE, which commemorates Horatio Nelson's naval victory over the French and Spanish Fleets in 1805. The square is dominated by the statue of Lord Nelson atop a 154-foot column.

Known mainly for its theaters, SHAFTESBURY AVENUE runs from New Oxford Street to Piccadilly Circus in the West End. Pictured is Cambridge Circus, where the avenue intersects Charing Cross Road (noteworthy for its bookstores). The Palace Theatre opened in 1891 as the English Opera House. Andrew Lloyd Webber, who owned the theater from 1982 to 2012, restored its terra-cotta facade and returned the lush interior to its former splendor.

Since the accession of Queen Victoria in 1837, BUCKINGHAM PALACE has been the London home of the reigning monarch. The east front of the palace was redesigned by Sir Aston Webb in 1913. Visitors can see the State Rooms at Buckingham Palace, but a more popular tourist attraction is the Changing the Guard in the forecourt. And each autumn, as part of another colorful pageant, the Queen is taken in the Irish State Coach to conduct the formal opening of Parliament. The procession passes the Queen Victoria Memorial outside Buckingham Palace and continues down the Mall and Whitehall to the House of Lords. There the Queen addresses members of Parliament.

A magnificently detailed structure covering eight acres, THE HOUSES OF PARLIAMENT were designed by Sir Charles Barry and built between 1840 and 1870, after a fire destroyed the old Palace of Westminster in 1834. The east facade extends for 940 feet along the Thames River. On the right, next to Westminster Bridge, is the Clock Tower. The complex of chambers, lobbies, and offices contains 100 staircases, 1,100 apartments, and two miles of passageways. Parliament consists of the Sovereign (King or Queen), the House of Lords, and the House of Commons. Its main function is making laws and governing the United Kingdom. The Commons Chamber, which was destroyed by bombs in 1941, reopened in 1950 after being rebuilt. In 1943, urging that the chamber be kept oblong and "not be big enough to contain all its Members at once without overcrowding," Winston Churchill said, "The vitality and the authority of the House of Commons and its hold upon an electorate . . . depends to no small extent upon its episodes and great moments, even upon its scenes and rows, which, as everyone will agree, are better conducted at close quarters."

Covering almost 18 acres, the TOWER OF LONDON consists of fortified walls, a moat (now a garden), and various other towers, barracks, and buildings. The oldest part, the White Tower, was built by William the Conquerer in the late 11th century as a symbol of his power and dominance over London. Having been variously used as a fortress, a royal residence, and a prison, the tower is now a popular tourist attraction. It contains the Crown Jewels, historic relics, and a magnificent collection of European armor and weapons. Displays include armor for a giant and a dwarf, as well as for an Indian elephant, probably the largest armor in the world. The Tower of London is open every day, but hours vary.

ST. PAUL'S CATHEDRAL was created by Sir Christopher Wren after the Great Fire of London in 1666. The central dome rises 365 feet above the ground. The cathedral itself is 515 feet long and 242 feet across, and is decorated with columns, porticoes, paintings, pediments, mosaics, and statuary. Circling the interior of the dome, accessible by stairs, is the Whispering Gallery. Words whispered into the wall on one side can clearly be heard on the other—112 feet away. The cathedral is open to sightseers every day except Sunday.